The Agile PMO

Leading the Effective, Value driven, Project Management Office

i

The Agile PMO

Third Edition © 2013 by Michael Nir

This publication is designed to provide accurate and authoritative information in regard to the subject matter covered. It is sold with the understanding that neither the Publisher nor the Author is engaged in rendering legal, accounting, or other professional service. If legal advice or other expert assistance is required, the services of a competent professional person should be sought. Neither the publisher nor the Author shall be liable for damages, directly or indirectly, arising herefrom.

The Agile PMO

The Agile PMO

Michael Nir

The Agile PMO

Preface

Congratulations! This book provides you with the **breakthrough professional knowledge** to grow your PMO NOW. Make your PMO pioneer the value driven efforts in the organization. It is based on valuable tested consulting experience and is now the foundation for a **popular keynote** presentation.

Join me in this journey to making your emerging PMO not only endure but also lead **project** and **portfolio** growth and be value driven: The PMO is a mediating function it enables visibility where there is shortsightedness, unity where there is disparity, transparency where there is ambiguity, and global breakthrough where there is only local analysis.

Over the years I have seen too many PMOs blunder and fail due to various misconceptions in the roll out and implementation. The main cause is that PMOs do not learn how to create true and substantial value for stakeholders from the portfolio perspective, and hence lose budgeting and are terminated; in this proven guide I will provide practical guidelines **with the assistance of a case study** on how to create and increase value of a PMO in an ever changing environment. Ultimately, after reading this guide you'll know what to do, in order to successfully and reliably lead your Agile PMO.

What readers say about this book:

*"Michael Nir writes a compelling a precisely structured piece about the common pitfalls of project management and the core rationale that should drive its successful implementation. In part this important topic is described and lifted with the aid of a case study; it should be practically compulsory for these challenging topics to come with case story data. It is a **fascinating read and certainly I agree with the points in this book that will be helpful** to project managers ..."*

*"..... The book refers to daily business rather than to scientific studies. So the reader is able to get a feeling where the PMO of his company is standing at the moment regarding the different types and weak points. Furthermore **the practical aspects especially the example really helped to understand that change is possible** (although it is hard and sometimes seems impossible) and has to be considered from all stakeholder's views and can be achieved by small steps like listing the projects and the critical resources. **The content was structured well** because in the beginning the different types of PMOs are mentioned followed by the problems PMOs have and in the end the PMO turns into a value adding one. In addition it was interesting to get an overview of Kotter's phases for change. **The book is a good motivator and provides help on how to change things.** ..."*

*"....**Michael's practical view based on company experience as opposed to theory** gets straight to the point. Add value from your stakeholders point of view is a neat, practical message that **Michael surrounds with ideas of how to do this** and takes the reader through a real case study...."*

*"....The eBook gives you a short insight into Michael's experience you could use when you have to set-up a PMO. The last section will give you **some best practices in creating a value driven PMO**. It uses Kotter's eight phases for change leadership to construct and maintain a value adding PMO. .... To explain this scenario Michael uses the same case as mentioned before..... If you are at the starting point of designing or implementing a PMO it's **definitely worthwhile reading and take these lessons into account...."***

*".....I am an experienced project manager and am in the process of implementing a PMO for a client and have struggled with getting buy-in to the process and governance (decision making). This book really helped remind me that we should be concentrating on the big picture - why is the PMO there - to add value in relation to resource management and delivering strategic projects. **Could not recommend it enough....***"*

*"....I wasn't originally looking for this book nor the topic, but when I noticed the book I was curious and purchased to read. The book was a quick ready but was **on point with my experiences as to why many PMO's have typically failed**. Which included becoming too focused on the methodology, passing papers, and not really delivering value. However, instead of focusing in on the failures, **Michael provides insights into how to implement and structure a successful PMO focusing on business outcomes and value..**"*

About the Author

Michael Nir has been providing operational, organizational and management training and consulting for over fourteen years. He is a certified project management professional and Gestalt process facilitator, offering training, consulting, and solutions development in project and product management, process improvement, leadership, and team building programs. Michael's background is analytical and technical; however, he has a keen interest in human interaction and behavior. He holds two engineering degrees from the prestigious Technion Institute of Technology: a Bachelor's of Civil engineering and a Master of Industrial engineering. He has balanced his technical aptitude with the extensive study and practice of Gestalt Therapy and Instrumental Enrichment, a philosophy of mediated learning. In his consulting and training engagements, Michael combines both the analytical and technical world with his focus on people, delivering unique and meaningful solutions, and addressing whole systems. His style is facilitative, favoring Socratic direction, employing a range of techniques, from mind mapping, NLP and accelerated learning to indoor gaming and active playful exercises. He has been working with a multitude of clients globally.

Preface to the 2nd edition

Agile project management and specifically scrum implementations have been gaining wide popularity in recent years. Along with the increasing out-of-the-box Scrum implementations there is growing discontent and disillusionment from agile project management approaches: As Most organizations maintain an overarching control mechanism that is represented in the waterfall methodology, the positioning and integration of Agile-Scrum is tricky. As a result, the initial rollout of Agile-Scrum which had been accompanied by enthusiasm and zeal was quickly replaced with dysfunction. This has been specifically apparent in the interface were the Agile-Scrum teams meet the traditional organizational control mechanisms.

While many books and articles are already aware of this discord, few words have been given on how to solve it. In the last chapter of this book I describe a best practice solution, based on consulting and implementation experience in complex environments. By positioning and defining proper roles and responsibilities, the agile PMO can be used to secure Agile-Scrum benefits whilst maintaining the necessary overarching control architecture. This creates a new and exciting role for the PMO which until recently might have been viewed as obsolete in Agile organizations.

Enjoy

Michael

Contents

The Agile PMO

Introduction – Authentic Failures

The story of PMO implementations in companies is a sad one. Initially there is a lot of excitement, there is a kickoff meeting and commitments are given, there are resources allocated to the new PMO and a budget is constructed. The new PMO manager is eager to proceed. He prepares a rollout plan, he gathers a team for some brainstorm sessions and he puts forth an impressive presentation detailing his plan. But even as he is doing this, the seeds of failure have already been sown.

It is a wonder that after 20 years of accumulated experience we are still making the same mistakes in implementing PMOs: We are still thinking of tools before process, we are still investigating process before methodology, and we are still emphasizing methodology before people:

1. Discussing tools before process is a grave error that leads to premature decisions concerning early investments, in what would be an inadequate solutions and a loss of support from required stakeholders;

2. Selecting a process before methodology makes the PMO lose sight of the big picture, thus forgoing the opportunity to implement one coherent approach of managing programs and portfolios;

3. Investing time in a methodology before leading the stakeholders and creating a strong support group for the PMO would ultimately result in a dysfunctional PMO.

The goal of each and every PMO is specifically: create value. A PMO creates value when and only when it enables educated fact-based decisions regarding resource allocation across projects, programs and portfolios. If subsequent to one year of inception, the PMO cannot provide an up-to-date accurate view of resource allocation then it has failed in the single most important role that a PMO has in the organization.

This is an important point to emphasize; after examination of PMO implementation in more than 100 organizations worldwide I maintain that the only reason for a PMO to exist is to create value. A PMO creates value by helping the organization decide where to invest its resources for the optimal return on investments. Tools, methodology, techniques, processes are all nice to have, however they do not constitute an objective in themselves. Value driven PMOs genuinely understand that they must continuously create, refine, and update the mapping of resource allocation in the organization. This is of course easier said than done, and most PMOs fall short of being able to produce such a representation.

Once the PMO understands what value is and the role it plays in creating value, it should follow the following three steps for implementation:

1. Kotter's eight phases of change management – chapter 7;
2. Continually being true to value – chapter 8;
3. The Agile PMO approach – delivering value incrementally – chapter 9.

Without following these prescribed steps, the PMO will likely fail, since it cannot and does not yield substantial value to the organization. At times the PMO becomes a tactical body or better described a secretarial office, maintaining status of projects and running errands for the project managers. Other times the PMO is disbanded altogether. Actually according to recent research by Gartner, around half of the PMOs are closed yearly.

Useful Guide Structure

This guide is structured in three sections, each section contains three chapters.

The first section introduces failures of PMOs. The first chapter portrays how the PMO can become a tactical governance body. In this situation the PMO might originally function as a value originator but as time goes by it becomes a tactical PMO. The second chapter discusses the methodology PMO, usually structured as such and not able to provide tangible value. The third chapter presents the PMO that provides a 'home' for project managers and is hardly a PMO at all in terms of value creation.

In the second section, misdirection of a value-based PMO is introduced through the use of a case study. The fourth chapter illustrates how PMOs that try to have the whole cake often fail. The fifth chapter illustrates how thinking in tools leads to the value-based PMO demise. The sixth chapter depicts how a PMO can easily make the life of project and product managers a nightmare by becoming a barrier to effective project management.

The third section describes how to construct and maintain a value adding PMO. The seventh chapter promotes change leadership during rollout and implementation as a key process for PMO success, and bases it on Kotter's eight phases for change leadership. The eighth chapter argues why it is important to be true to value, and what it means to be an effective PMO. The ninth chapter introduces the concept of the Agile PMO which delivers only what is necessary at the proper time. The tenth chapter is a new supplement to the second edition illustrating the role of the Agile PMO in a hybrid Agile-Scrum and Linear-Waterfall organization.

Section 1 – Colossal Failures of PMOs

The first chapter portrays how the PMO can become a tactical administrative entity. In this situation the PMO might originally function as a value originator but with time it develops features tactical. The second chapter discusses the methodology PMO, usually structured as such and unable to provide tangible value. The third chapter presents the PMO that provides a 'home' for project managers and is hardly a PMO at all in terms of value creation.

Note, these three classifications of three different types of PMOs are a generalization and simplification of real world PMOs. Most PMOs would be a combination of these three types. Some PMOs would tend to be more tactical but still provide methodological support, while others might provide a home for project managers and methodological support while not being tactical at all. The easiest way to examine the PMO in your organization is to ask the stakeholders what type of interaction and support they receive from the PMO. Also note, based on many surveys that we have carried out, it is unlikely that the stakeholders will associate the PMO with notions of value creation.

Thinking Alert - Are you a member of a PMO? Is there a PMO in your organization? Can you classify your PMO into any of the above categories? Write down your impressions and experiences with the daily and weekly functions of your PMO, identify the key activities of your PMO and categorize them – are you able to define the value your PMO provides?

Chapter 1 – The Tactical PMO

The tactical PMO is not established by intent as tactical. Normally, upon inception it is viewed as a value generator. Initially, the hopes are high for a governing body that enables:

1. Control of projects;
2. Visibility of project status;
3. Portfolio-based decisions;
4. An overall improvement of project management practices.

The most notable reason for the implementation of such a PMO is: lack of visibility of project work throughout the portfolios, projects and programs. Moreover the organization's project structure is often a shambles, and control and monitor mechanisms are missing. This often occurs when the organization is undergoing fast growth. Accompanying this growth is an increasing number of projects managed concurrently. Management feels that it is losing its control on the projects; this feeling is exacerbated by possible diminishing returns in the existing projects. The need for a quick fix is evident.

The PMO in this arrangement is hastily constructed to provide the solution. However the PMO is announced without time for proper analysis and lacking true understanding of the means through which the PMO can increase value to the organization. Management and project sponsors are searching for immediate portfolio control as well as a response to the project management deficiencies the organization has been experiencing. Usually the PMO manager is nominated without proper background check. Sometimes, a lead volunteer from the project organization is selected to head the PMO. As the new head eases into his new role he understands that it will be difficult and even next to impossible to create the reporting structure within the current company processes. In order to circumvent timesheet reporting issues, lack of appropriate software tools, lack of a methodology, lack of processes, and above all an army of resistance both from the project community and from the resource and technical community, he opts for tactical tracking of resource usage by and through the PMO.

The PMO manager nominates administrative staff and analysts to act as super secretaries for the project managers.

These super secretaries as their name implies perform the menial tasks of project management such as:

1. Collect data;
2. Write down project plans;
3. Manage project issues;
4. Summarize meetings.

Moreover, they perform duties which the project managers themselves prefer to avoid. Ironically this behavior leads to the PMO demise.

The above described scenario might also occur in technology oriented organizations where project managers perceive themselves beyond handling administrative tasks and therefore push back against management request for comprehensive management of the projects. Since planning, risk management, monitoring and controlling of the projects are necessary, the PMO fills this role. Actually, the PMO faces an army of resistance from the project management community. They do not wish to be troubled with project management at all and tend to ridicule the profession in general, therefore remaining uncooperative with all the PMO activities. In these organizations, this sentiment is shared also by executives. The PMO is not able to withstand this lack of sponsorship; the result is a downgraded PMO performing technical function as described.

This is not to say that value-based PMOs do not provide project managers with support of managing the projects. Actually, good PMOs are able to provide value to project managers as they are managing the project. Indeed a PMO can and should assist with project planning, risk management, summary of meetings, and issue management as part of the value driven approach. The concern is that in some situations the PMO handles *only* such errands and does not live out to be a strategic body enabling portfolio selection and overall management across the organization. Being totally immersed in the daily activities of projects, the PMO cannot lift up its head so to speak, and engage in more important value enabling activities.

Summarizing, the tactical PMO is usually compelled by the powerful project organization to maintain only tactical functions and not to support value-added activities. Some would argue that there is nothing wrong with a tactical PMO, however tactical PMOs are destined to fail. Once funds diminish, and management is aware that it does not receive a valid depiction of project and portfolio status, it rightly questions the continuation of PMO budgeting. As a result, PMO resources are removed and the project managers must once more manage the administrative aspects of their projects.

Some organizations I have worked with employ project analysts who function as tactical project administrators. A specific defense industry company has a big team of students and junior engineers providing them with project planning and monitoring for the senior project managers. Since the company is operating in a high margin market, the added costs of maintaining this luxury are easily absorbed by the business units.

I have also witnessed organizations where the PMO personal is drawn to perform tactical project management. Since people are measured by their perceived efficiency and since the daily activity of projects have high visibility, PMO personal are lured to perform the menial tasks of project management, to demonstrate their indispensableness – it is this behavior that often undermines their   true effectiveness. When the funds diminish, they are the first to be dismissed.

Chapter 2 – The Methodology PMO

> **Methodology**: 'a body of methods, rules, and postulates employed by a discipline : a particular procedure or set of procedures.'

> **Method:** 'a way, technique, or process of or for doing something.'

> **Process:** 'a series of actions or operations conducing to an end; *especially* : a continuous operation or treatment especially in manufacture.'

> Definitions from: the free *Merriam-Webster dictionary*

> *A methodology consists of methods which in turn consist of processes.*

The methodology PMO is often established in mature organizations where there is a need to provide additional structure for projects and programs. Stakeholders note that they have either a multitude of tools, techniques, procedures, templates and work instructions but lack governance in the usage of these tools, or alternatively there are no such tools in project or product development. Hence, a PMO is chartered and sponsored. The PMO's charter includes mapping of the required methodology to be properly implemented, together with management's blessing to proceed. The PMO leader is a mature project manager usually tired of managing projects, a senior quality manager, or a new totally fresh resource from other business units in the organization. His plans for methodology implementation most likely fall on deaf ears as the project managers are convinced that there is nothing wrong with the way they are handling their projects. During formal meetings there is an outward acceptance of the requests made by the PMO, but otherwise there is no implementation of the methodology, processes, and work instructions, proposed and developed by the PMO.

At times when management dictates the usage of the approaches mandated by the PMO, a double reporting mechanism springs into existence. On the one hand the reluctant project managers comply with the requests and complete all the necessary documentation; on the other hand there is no authentic integration between the methodology promoted by the PMO and the way the project is managed. It is normal to witness two levels of project execution in this case. The formal execution of the project as displayed in the templates which the project managers hand to the PMO for governance, and the actual execution of the project as displayed in the actual daily activities of the project. This dual reporting mechanism translates to increased project risk - as the gap between formal plans and actual execution will most likely lead to failed expectations.

The project managers often complain and grumble against this dual layer reporting mechanism, to anyone who cares to listen. Indeed in this scenario the load and burden on the project managers is double, with no value created.

In several organizations which had global presence and over 10,000 employees worldwide we witnessed the negative impacts of the methodology PMO. The project managers failed to prioritize between delivering value to the organization by advancing project activities, and formally filling out templates to comply with the PMO mandated methodology. Moreover, the project managers who complied with the formal requirements of the PMO were the one that received the benefits from senior stakeholders while the project managers who contributed to the organization's success through project performance were often rebuked for not complying with organization standards; this might sound counterintuitive, however many times organizations measure employees by compliance rather than for achievements.

It is important to emphasize that methodology, process, work instructions, and templates are important for completing projects on time, within budget and according to the defined scope and level of quality; however PMOs which are founded on implementing a methodology are necessarily flawed as their focus would be on promoting their defined agenda. As the PMO leader will be measured on his success of implementing a methodology, he will invest his energies towards that end.

Generally speaking, once there is a defined business entity whose role and goal is specific, it will for sure promote that goal without consideration for the overall business perspective. It is similar to the famous saying "the bureaucracy is expanding to meet the needs of the expanding bureaucracy" (Q. Wilde). This is the reason that a PMO which is focused on implementing a methodology is destined to fail. Methodology is a means and not an end. At times it seems that organizations confuse between the means of having a methodology and the goal of completing projects. Similar to the tactical PMO, once funds are depleted and no tangible value is produced the PMO will be disbanded.

Note: I have seen PMOs who implement a full-fledged methodology based on PMI's PMBOK® consisting of numerous processes, templates, tools and techniques and work instructions. They had brought great agony to the project organization, increasing overhead without contributing tangible value. It is sometimes awkward to accept being an administrative burden, since by acknowledging you are admitting your insignificance. The remedy is simple though – focus on value creation.

Thinking Alert – which methodology do you have in place in your organization for project realization? Can you define the value gained from the methodology? How encumbering is it? How much red tape is embodied in the methodology? Is it a – one size fits all project management methodology, or are there variations for the methodology based on project characteristics? Can you possibly relax elements of the methodology and obtain the same results?

While some structure is necessary, PMO's can often reduce project management process overhead by more than 25%, contributing to faster project delivery. The rule is – if you can't provide concrete reasoning for a certain process and template – then it is waste and should be removed.

Chapter 3 – The Project Manager Home PMO

The PMO can serve as the project manager's functional base, in this setting, the project managers are managed by the PMO manager. It is not necessarily a bad arrangement, as the PMO can assist the project managers more closely when they are his/her direct reports. The snag is that often the PMO manager expects the project managers in this structure to participate in PMO activities and to contribute to the methodology, processes, templates and work instructions on top of their project duties. As the project managers are tight for time as it is, they find little availability for promoting anything but their projects. This PMO structure is mostly apparent in technological organizations with limited funds.

It is rare to find a PMO whose sole purpose is to act as the home for the project managers. In terms of organizational investment, this is the least expensive PMO as the only investment required is to aggregate all project managers under an organization unit and assign them a manager. The organization and PMO manager expect the project managers to contribute outside their project activities and to promote various aspects of the PMO. The project managers depending on their seniority will push back on management's requirement and will ask for additional support. The additional support might be from a junior administrative assistant or a junior industrial engineer, who will tend to the many tasks of the PMO. As value is not even considered, this type of PMO can exist for a long time without being discarded. At times, this structure is used for mentoring and coaching young project managers joining the organization, by having them accompany a senior project manager on a project. It is quite useful in this respect, as it is promoting knowledge transfer and on the job training. On top of that, sharing of information can occur in this structure between all project managers contributing to project success. This PMO type can become a center of excellence.

The PMO that aggregates project managers into one organization unit and serves as the project manager 'home' can sometimes have organizational units reporting to it. It is not uncommon in big global organizations to have the PMO act as a program management office, managing several lower-level project management offices across several regions. In this case the PMO is not intended to create value, methodology, and gathering of project information; rather this structure is merely a method to organize resources in the overall organization. Thus naming an organizational unit a PMO can be misleading in terms of the expectation of the output to be provided by that specific unit.

While there isn't a major drawback in having a PMO act as a home to the project managers, it is often difficult for this PMO to focus on value creation. Value creation in portfolio management, entails resource and project prioritization. This in turn calls for a level of objectivity from the PMO team, to select and prioritize projects based on unbiased criteria. The independent analysis is challenged when the

PMO team includes active project managers. One can imagine the conflict they are facing when required to optimally assign resources to projects irrespective of the projects they themselves mange.

Section 2 – Remarkable Mis-directions of a Value Based PMOs

This section introduces a case study, which describes a global telecommunication company that sells to original equipment manufacturers (OEM), developing both hardware and software. The company has just acquired a development site in Bangalore India where software projects are managed. The company has seen exponential growth in the number of projects it is managing, and assigned the PMO to create a standard approach for project management. The company has 80 project managers distributed among 15 sites: seven in North America, four in Europe and four in Asia and Australia. Some of these project managers are marketing project managers, others work in new project integration into operations, and the majority of project managers work in development. Naturally the project managers report to their relevant business unit. The corporate offices in North America have mandated the inception of a PMO, which will globally manage the company's project and program portfolio. Tom Jenkins, a senior project manager has been appointed head PMO and recruited three junior employees from various departments, each with up to three years of experience.

With support from Tom and his PMO team, the fourth chapter illustrates how PMOs that try to have the whole cake often fail. The fifth chapter shows how thinking in tools leads to the value-based

PMO demise. The sixth chapter depicts how a PMO can easily make the life of project managers a nightmare by becoming a barrier to effective project management.

Chapter 4 – Biting at the Whole Cake (and chocking)

Tom has recently been appointed to lead the newly formed PMO. His first order of business was to analyze current company processes. He interviewed over 15 project managers from three of the 15 sites. He met with many stakeholders to understand their concerns and requirements of the new PMO. Being quite senior in the company with over 18 years of experience, he had access to many stakeholders which helped him map the challenges the company is facing. He noticed a discrepancy between the various sites in the methods and tools that projects were utilizing. Specifically the approach for planning was different between sites and the software development lifecycle that was widely used in development across Europe was nonexistent in Asia and different than the one used in America. Risk management was done superficially. Projects were using a myriad of processes and templates for estimating, scheduling, budgeting, and controlling the projects. Resource assignments were not visible, it was impossible to know who was working when on what; as such the portfolio selection process was rudimentary. Many "pet" projects existed, many seemingly low benefit projects were in the pipeline, and value generated projects were late because they were missing critical resources.

Tom decided to divide the work among three PMO junior analysts; he assigned Paula Benua the development of a methodology. He gave responsibilities to Xing Yoshin to carry out the full-fledged process analysis as well responsibility for timesheet reporting of the entire portfolio. Xavier Popendoz was responsible for coordinating the unification of the tools and techniques throughout the global organization. In six months Tom and his team were ready to introduce the new way of work. With much fanfare and pyrotechnics the team displayed the new software development lifecycle composed of seven phase gates, 21 new processes for project and product management, and 30 supporting templates. A new timesheet reporting structure was put in place and a governance process was established to support it.

Needless to say that while this initiative was greeted with enthusiasm by key stakeholders; it was received with a pinch of anxiety from project, product and resource managers. In the next three months SharePoint sites for departments were rolled out and virtual training sessions were conducted to educate the global organization with the newly approved way of work. The project managers started to use some of the new tools, however couldn't catch up with all the new methods. Each project manager and team chose what they thought was most relevant; while some actually completely ignored the initiative, hoping it will blow away. Amazed with the low level of conformity to the new way of work, the PMO escalated to management, which enlisted the support of functional and resource managers. They were ordered to force compliance on all their direct reports. Even this provided little help, as the managers themselves were reluctant to ensure utilization of the new way of work; they felt that it was just too much. One element of the new way of work was successfully enforced. This was the weekly actual effort reporting which was the cornerstone in the new portfolio management tool. Resources were required to capture their daily project work and log them at least weekly in the system. The PMO monitored completion of these logs and sent weekly alerts to the resources. Those who didn't comply were warned and then reprimanded if continued to ignore the reminders. The resulting portfolio report based on actual efforts was colorful and impressive – and became an important element in the portfolio management dashboard. The executive stakeholder rejoiced, and rumor spread that during the executive yearly offsite strategic planning sessions, it was decided to change the dashboard indicator, for late and troubled projects, from red to burgundy – as homage to the broken bottle of 1972 Pinar, red wine, that was accidently spilled on the president during the annual executive Golf tournament.

One year later, it came as quite a surprise that timesheet showing theoretical efforts but were far from reflecting resource usage. Projected costs as displayed in the dashboard didn't explain actual project costs which had been 20%
inspection carried out by the PMO team revealed that the
were maintaining their pre-implementation way of work. Out of the 21 new processes only 5 were fully integrated. Frustrated and

defeated, Tom moved to France, pursuing his long life dream, he acquired a vineyard in Burgundy. In an ironic twist of fate his first yield was too red to be considered suitable for the Burgundy wines.

The case study demonstrates the impact of aiming for full-fledged implementation in a global organization. Often what transpires is a colossal failure, the saying 'grasp all - lose all' is an apt description. The high profile PMO roll out, characterized by a seemingly supportive management team usually leads to a high profile PMO failure. It might appear that the full implementation is necessary since the PMO manager is eager to show immediate extensive success, which is exacerbated by expectations from senior management. An in-depth scrutiny reveals that the PMO manager places himself in a predicament by over selling and creating high executive expectations which are unrealistic. What more, much of what the PMO is promising is actually **non value added elements** in the overall project management methodology. The resulting failure is almost guaranteed. On top of that, little is done to manage fears and resistance from the project organization and the overall atmosphere is one of dictation and not of collaboration. Consulting firms assisting in the PMO rollout can worsen the situation by pushing for implementation of theoretical best practices as opposed to analysis of the current state and organization-specific requirements.

Summarizing, the full-fledged head-on PMO implementation approach, more often fails then succeeds, resulting in wasted efforts, budgets and trust.

Thinking Alert – create an Excel (or any other spreadsheet) table of the project management processes, tools, techniques, and templates which exist within your organization. Group these into categories such as Risk management, product related (design), planning management, estimating and scheduling, budgeting, etc. define the importance – clarify whether these are value added, non-value added and required non value added. Simulate what might happen if you skip a certain process, tool, technique or template. Maybe you can simplify or integrate? Ask for support from other people in analyzing your company's way of work.

Chapter 5 – Thinking in Tools and loosing Perspective

The case study presented in the previous chapter is also used in this chapter in a different scenario. In this instance, Xavier is responsible for PMO tool development.

Xavier was extremely pleased; he had just finished a thorough analysis of existing off the shelf enterprise portfolio management (EPM) software tools, and was ready to present his findings to his boss and to senior management. For four months since the PMO inception, Xavier had been very busy collecting requirements, analyzing options, and discussing with global IT the various choices for EPM implementation. He had shortlisted three market-leading candidates to replace several tools for managing projects and portfolios currently in place in the global organization. He was convinced that the only way to solve the misalignment between the different regions' project and product management approaches was by implementing a common ubiquitous enterprise portfolio management solution. He summarized the requirements from the software in a presentation and listed the characteristics and options which the solution must have to answer the requirements (in no specific order of importance) as seen below.

Detailed EPM requirements list:

1. Built in reports capability;
2. Export to anywhere from everywhere;

3. Predefined alert mechanism;

4. Support critical chain and agile approaches;

5. Be compatible with all software development lifecycle;

6. Tweak data in every way that we might like;

7. Easy to understand GUI;

8. Advanced coloring mechanisms;

9. Easy to understand;

10. Templates that answer all our needs and all the available formats, also enabling filtering, grouping, aggregating and sorting;

11. On the fly permission management;

12. Totally scalable;

13. Fully integrated budget, cost and time reporting;

14. Easy to implement timesheets with interface to mobile technology;

15. Fully integrated with all existing tools;

16. Easy to customize.

Xavier was somewhat taken aback initially by the numerous requirements defined by the stakeholders. However, being the diligent analyst that he was, with three years of management consulting experience in one of the world's leading firms – 'Appleson', he immediately applied Pareto analysis to the requirements. Following an in-depth structuring exercise he came to the conclusion that Pareto analysis was not useful, and moved to prioritize the full list of software requirements. He implemented a sophisticated pair-wise comparison for prioritization of the requirements, also known as Satty, and was surprised to see that on a 1 to 5 scale all requirements received a grade of one, meaning all were highly important to the stakeholders. He then moved to consult Lawrence, his old boss, a senior partner with 'Appleson consulting and sons'. Lawrence listened carefully and then suggested that he meet with Tom Jenkins - the PMO leader to persuade him to take Appleson consulting for this project. Xavier was flabbergasted; he really liked Lawrence and was thrilled with the idea of teaming up with his old colleagues at Appleson. Lawrence was already preparing a draft agreement for professional services.

Tom, however, was not fond of this idea and suggested that Xavier run a multi regression – variable prioritization technique on the list of EPM software requirements that he gathered. After due analysis, Xavier was finally successful and was able to remove two requirements from the list. These were seemingly minor requirements requested by the development team in Melbourne Australia that had to do with synchronization of the clock when updating schedule information into the servers. Xavier was delighted to present his shorter list in the colorful presentation that he constructed.

Subsequently, management decided on investing in 'EPM-metrics' a powerful enterprise portfolio management solution from a think tank organization devoted to project management. The initial upfront investment was at the $300,000 mark, not including customization and seven on-site software engineers for two years support.

Again, the rollout of the software was accompanied with much fanfare. The pilot implementation consisted of core teams at the various regions, and the quick internet and mobile access was actualized and tested. The teams were required to report using the snazzy user interface. Everyone was very happy. The internal software database engine integrated the various regions' formats, churning them, producing a colorful aggregated display.

The roll out continued, however major issues started resurfacing; ten months into the full fledged implementation, it was evident that the software engine was not able to support four different software development life cycles from the different regions, five different budgeting approaches, separate reporting mechanisms, 15 different templates for documenting meetings, four approaches for risk management, and approximately 30 special dashboards. It was also noted that there was some challenge with clock synchronization between Australia and the rest of the world. In order to resolve this issue an additional $230,000 would have to be invested.

While the above scenario might seem somewhat extreme, it illustrates what occurs when an organization decides to move forward with tool selection and implementation before reaching a common understanding concerning methodology, processes and templates.

PMOs who invest in an EPM software tool prior to reaching consensus concerning the appropriate methodology are destined to fail.

From the field: I recently participated in a PPM tool selection meeting with one of my clients. This client had a mature PMO and indeed it was the appropriate time to select a software solution. While I consulted the client with several aspects of the PMO, I wasn't involved in the tool selection process and was invited to join the laer stages of the proof of concept. The three software vendors, or solution providers as they prefer to be called, were thoroughly ready to demonstrate the capabilities and were doing a great job. The challenge was the breadth of requirements provided by irrelevant stakeholders who insisted on participating in the meeting. It seems that there is lack of understanding of what a PPM solution can provide. Digressing somewhat from our topic I would like to offer my perspective. There are two orthogonal axes by which one can assess PPM software:

- The portfolio-project scheduling engine axis
- The level customizability - 'open' API axis

The portfolio-project scheduling engine axis: EPM products usually have roots in one of two: either the original product is a project scheduling tool where EPM functionality has been built on top, or the core original product is a portfolio management tool where the project scheduling model has been built into it. Most available EPM products provide a robust solution for one and an Ok solution for the other. For example Microsoft project ® is at its core a scheduling tool. The scheduling tool that Microsoft has is great for effort based resource management and resource pool scheduling. The server which has been built on top, and incidentally is most likely not in Microsoft road map for future development, is to this day quite limited with portfolio management functionalities. It is crucial that stakeholders understand the key functionality they are looking for in the tool and align their expectations with what the tool truly offers.

The level customizability - 'open' API axis: some products have easy to access application programming interfaces and are highly customizable, others are less flexible and not as customizable. As a general rule of thumb, the more rigid the product, the faster the initial rollout and the more expensive the tool is. Companies find the rigid tools inadequate only when they start exploring fulfilling the complex requirements usually a year subsequent to initial implementation. These complex requirements necessitate the purchase of an off the shelf commercial add-on, or expensive development. Customizable EPM products are initially cheaper to purchase, and more difficult to roll out. The many flavors and possibilities allow too many degrees of freedom to the stakeholders. Some companies are overwhelmed by these, and as a result the PMO revises and updates constantly the solution, resulting in endless bugs and fixes. The initial cheaper cost is sometimes offset by the frequent software customization.

Using the grid we can analyze our requirements, easily translating them into the context of the two axes. Indeed, I am aware of Gartner's magic quadrant for analyzing PPM tools. As a supplement to Gartner's grid the above described tool assists in analyzing the stakeholders' requirements and categorizing them into one of the four areas in the tool; this assisting in proper tool selection.

Chapter 6 – The obstacle-creating PMO – A true blunder

Using the same case study we will now explore another scenario which is a variation on the fourth chapter – biting too much. In this instance, Paula (who is responsible for PMO methodology) and Tom have implemented a robust software development lifecycle methodology.

The software development lifecycle (SDLC) was based on a linear approach, specifically the Waterfall methodology. The overall methodology included a comprehensive suite of:

1. Seven phase gates for reviews;
2. Three design review processes;
3. A design transfer process;
4. A design change mechanism;
5. An overall approach for integrating product requirements into project rollout;
6. Numerous templates for project planning.

The structured approach was very logical and practical. The PMO team was proud to provide such an extensive and comprehensive solution that would probably solve the many annoying issues that plagued project and product development. In order to implement this approach, new roles in the various regions were identified and responsibilities assigned. Initially, the complete package was received with the blessing from the project and product community. However, as some project were moving into the later phases of testing it was evident that the overall SDLC architecture was too cumbersome for the testing approach that was practiced within the organization.

Prior to the implementation of the new waterfall approach, the testing phase was a combination of iterative bug fixing with daily communication and interfacing with the client, resembling a hybrid Agile approach. The new methodology mandated a more formal collaboration with the client, and distanced the client and user community from the testing process. This lengthened product development and to an extent aggravated both the clients and the project managers. Since the PMO has appointed local resources that verified implementation according to the new procedure it was difficult for the testing team, project managers, and clients to bypass the mandated process. An outcry for the implementation of an accepted agile development lifecycle spread from the project and product community. However it did not reach senior management and instead increased tension between local PMO representatives and the development community. Senior management was annoyed as the projects were behind schedule and the clients were unhappy. Overtime bug fixing was mandated, and the project teams were asked to invest extra effort and work longer and harder to produce results. Several key developers left the company over a short period, which obviously negatively impacted completion dates.

The PMO maintained that projects were behind schedule, over budget and delivering partial scope, since project and resource managers were not following the guidelines as defined in the waterfall SDLC. Tom and Paula collected evidence to support these assertions. During an important global videoconference they presented their findings and received continued support for their position, mainly due to the fact that upper management loved the colorful dashboards that they were receiving weekly. The PMO also demonstrated through timesheet analysis that the amount of effort and bug fixing has recently increased and implicitly blamed the business analysts for not eliciting user requirements correctly. While PMO personnel had been thoroughly ready for the meeting, the project and product managers had little time to occupy themselves with data gathering as they were continuously working overtime to complete the projects and releasing the products. After the VP for product development in the Americas had to step down, the new VP was able to secure resources and budget for a piloted Agile implementation.

Does this scenario sound familiar; have you seen such challenges in your organization? PMOs can at times create barriers for proper project and product development. In this scenario, the challenge is not the amount of new processes and tools that the PMO released; rather it is the methodology (such as a Project management lifecycle) implemented which is too foreign and incompatible with the existing way of work. Moreover, instead of assuming the role of a mediator and a partner, the PMO alienates itself from the project and product community.

In general there exists an initial distrust in most organizations between the newly incepted PMO and the project community. Project managers tend to view the PMO suspiciously as in its implicit role description, it create administrative burden that impacts project managers workload. A PMO that is too keen on representing management instead of supporting the product development efforts is increasing the collaboration challenges rather than alleviating them.

Summarizing this section; there are many ways a PMO can eradicate value. The above example scenarios within the case study are in fact true stories that have occurred in organizations. Trying to carry out the opposite of what is presented in these case studies is not necessarily the proper method to construct a value driven PMO.

The following section will introduce best practices in creating a value driven PMO. Striking a balance between control requirements from upper-level management on the one hand and support for the project and product community on the other hand, is vital in achieving value creation.

Thinking Alert: the PMO has to attain a certain level of support from the project community to succeed in creating value to the organization. A swift method to assess the level of rapport the PMO has with the project community is through a survey. Most PMOs avoid collecting information about their perceived performance. Arguably, as the PMO is an organizational support function, it makes absolute sense to assess the PMO by carrying out a 360 appraisal.

When in fact we had carried out surveys for troubled PMOs – it was not surprising to discover that the project and product community as a whole were viewing the respective PMOs as an interference to project and product delivery and as a waste of time and effort. On top of that, not one survey described the PMO as a portfolio management entity geared towards value driven project and program selection and prioritization. These are troubling news indeed. I highly recommend carrying out anonymous surveys to assess your PMO as a basis for improvement.

Some questions we use in our surveys are:

- Please describe your interaction with the PMO.
- In your point of view – what is the role of the PMO in the organization?
- Is the PMO fulfilling its role?
- Is the PMO necessary to complete projects on time, within the budget and according to the defined scope?
- How is the PMO contributing to project and product completion?
- What is the value that the PMO contributes to the organization?

- Can you provide ideas on how the PMO can increase its value?

The above questions can be open or close ended. The survey can include both types of questions. I recommend a mix. I also recommend piloting the survey prior to general submission in order to assess the possible answers. As I mentioned before, there is usually a rift between the project and product community and the PMO, so survey results can be quite nasty. I am surprised to hear repeatedly, participants in the workshops I lead complain vehemently about the PMOs in their organizations. The criticism is varied, however the underlining theme is that the PMOs have little understanding of the real mechanics of project and product delivery and are usually occupied with **non value added activities**. Having said that, bear in mind that while a certain level of discontent is expected, if the rift is actually a chasm, the PMO has to rethink its position and invest more time around Kotter's steps for change management – as described in the next chapter.

If the PMO can't prove on a daily basis that his performance is linked to value creation – his days are numbered.

Section 3 – Ultimately - how to construct and maintain a value adding PMO

The third section presents the remedies to the various syndromes described previously; the seventh chapter promotes change leadership during rollout and implementation as a key process for PMO success and bases it on Kotter's eight phases for change leadership. The eighth chapter argues why it is important to be true to value, and what it means to be an effective PMO. The ninth chapter introduces the concept of the Agile PMO which delivers only what is necessary at the proper time. The tenth chapter explores the model of the PMO as an interface between Agile / Scrum teams and Waterfall.

Chapter 7 – Breakthrough Change Leadership

This chapter describes the importance of change leadership. It introduces Kotter's model of eight phases of change leadership. Naturally, implementation of the PMO is a change process and therefore should be managed accordingly. Kotter's model is used as a guide and framework for this chapter. It is interesting to note that Kotter's model while widely known and accepted in the soft skill community such as human resource departments, is not well-known within the engineering /hard skills domain such as development, IT, operations, etc. This is a shame as most projects, whether product development projects, IT projects, and similar efforts that are considered hard skills domain, are principally change processes and would benefit from employing Kotter's change leadership model.

Kotter had studied more than 100 companies undergoing change and found common mistakes made during the change process. Among these are: being too complacent; failing to create a coalition; not developing a clear vision; not communicating the vision transparently; missing on short-term wins; perceiving that the change has been completed too soon; and failing to anchor changes in the corporate culture.

Kotter's eight phases of change is a systematic approach to achieving and promoting change by decomposing the change process into eight phases. The first three are all about creating a climate for change. The next two on engaging and enabling the organization. And the last three, implementing and sustaining change. From experience we learn that successful change occurs when there is commitment, a sense of urgency or momentum, stakeholder engagement, openness, clear vision, good and clear communication, strong leadership, and a well executed plan. Kotter's 8-step change model recognizes each of these characteristics.

Kotter emphasizes the need for leadership in change, as leaders define the future, align people with that future (note the usage of people and not resources), and inspire people to pursue that future. In summary: Kotter's eight phases of change provide a framework for systematically leading the change process, enabling people to bring lasting changes within their respective organization and avoiding fatal mistakes along the way.

Kotter's eight phases for change leadership are:

1. Establish a sense of urgency;
2. Create a coalition;
3. Develop clear vision;
4. Share the vision;
5. Empower people to clear obstacles;
6. Secure short-term wins;
7. Consolidate and keep moving;
8. Anchor change.

Kotter emphasizes the importance of following the model to the letter, without skipping steps, as described below.

1. Create a Sense Of Urgency – Kotter maintains that for a change to be successful, the change leadership team needs to communicate to the stakeholder community the importance of the change. The change leadership team should analyze the causes which necessitate the change, creating a compelling statement which persuades the stakeholders to support it. The message portrays the possible impact of what might transpire if the change is not implemented. This message should be articulated in quantitative visual means to increase its impact. Normally the establishment of a PMO in itself creates the required sense of urgency. More often than not the PMO will be established as a result of a crisis or a potential crisis. However, as the PMO is founded it is vital to also communicate the initial sense of urgency.

2. Create a Coalition - in order to instill the change, a critical mass of change supporters must lead it. As the PMO is rolled out and during the subsequent weeks, the PMO team should analyze stakeholders using a stakeholder assessment tool such as a power and interest grid. With this tool, stakeholders are analyzed according to their perceived interest in the change, and their power to impact the change process. Usually this will be translated into a four quadrant grid, containing:

1.   High power high interest stakeholders;

2. High power low interest stakeholders;
3. Low power high interest stakeholders;
4. Low power low interest stakeholders.

The next step is to assign stakeholders to one of the following groups

1. Proponents (those supporting the change);
2. Neutral (those indifferent to the change);
3. Opponents (those opposing the change).

A strong leading coalition is made of those high power high interest proponents as well as some high power low interest proponents. At times the PMO team would find it difficult to locate supporters and would need to think creatively in order to develop the team of proponents. The members of this team must recognize the value of the change and share trust and commitment.

Beware: This is the first out of three neglected steps in PMO implementations. While the PMO receives support from management, the PMO team is not investing time and effort in analyzing the possible threats to the implementation from the project and product community. Moreover, possible support from stakeholders, other than management, is overlooked which will in later phases of the implementation prove to be detrimental. The guiding coalition is an important enabler of change, and a crucial pillar in successful change efforts.

3. Create Vision and Strategy - a clear vision is vital in leading a change. The vision provides a bridge between the as-is (present) and to-be (future) states. The vision provides a sense of direction and helps aligning efforts. Useful visions tend to be SMART; Specific, Measurable, Attainable, Realistic, and Time-bound.

PMOs might already believe that they have a clear vision which is based on the mandated charter given by management; they could not be more mistaken. The PMO vision should relate to the near and long term objectives and instill a sense of pride. It is useful to combine mission with the vision, though it is not mandatory. Strategy description is also vital as it will outline the steps that lead to the vision.

The typical vision statement offered by a PMO would be similar to the following:

> *The mission of the Project Management Office (PMO) is to provide an enterprise-wide approach to identify, prioritize, and successfully execute a technology portfolio of initiatives and projects that are aligned with the LONDEC* strategic goals and educational vision...*

*Londec – an imaginary company used in my keynote presentation which describes the concepts of this book.

PMOs are quite adept at providing a concise vision statement that clarifies their role and their vision of the future state.

4. Communicate the Change Vision - it is crucial to communicate the vision to stakeholders to create understanding and commitment to the change. Failing to communicate the vision or alternatively being inconsistent with the communicated messages is a major risk which can lead to a failed change effort. A PMO that speaks in more than one voice damages the clear vision and instills uncertainty among stakeholders. The communication should be adjusted to the different stakeholders; the previously mentioned stakeholder assessment grid can be used as a basis for communication planning, as follows:

1. High power high interest stakeholders should be managed closely;
2. High power low interest stakeholders should be kept satisfied;
3. Low power high interest stakeholders should be kept informed;
4. Low power low interest stakeholders should be monitored loosely.

A communication plan for the change can be established following the above guidelines. A PMO can use a well formatted newsletter for communication with stakeholders; one cannot underestimate the effectiveness of using a newsletter in an organization. In many organizations, pertinent information regarding change initiatives is not freely shared; this in turn creates rumors, misinformation and miscommunication. PMO teams, who are advertising the change plans using a newsletter, are sending a powerful message to the stakeholder community. The newsletter will also be beneficial for later phases of the rollout. In general, the newsletter assists in branding the PMO and positioning it as a change agent and as a mediator between management and the project and product community.

Note: Newsletter can be either push or pull communication. I highly recommend using both methods: sending the newsletter as an email as well as sharing it as part of the PMO intranet site. This requires managing two formats which increases the invested effort, yet it guarantees maximum visibility. During early phases of roll out, it is vital that the newly formed PMO receives as much publicity as possible.

5. Empower People - the powerful coalition of proponents has to remove obstacles that are embedded in the organization structure, processes, or existing solely in the perception of employees. The PMO must instill a sense of empowerment throughout the project and product community. The goal is that employees feel they are playing a contributing part in the overall initiative. The PMO can use the newsletter to advertise achievements by employees in one area of the organization to the entire project and product community, thereby empowering and creating visibility and significance to these achievements and employees.

Beware: This is the second out of three neglected steps in PMO implementations. PMOs tend to keep the cards to themselves so to speak. They carry out the change initiatives unaided, and avoid trusting the people outside the PMO to assist them with roll out and implementation. They often treat the project and product community as a homogenous team of adversaries without harnessing active support from individuals who might later become agents of change. There is much to be said concerning the perceived distrust between the PMO team which represents the top down control mechanism as dictated by management and the project and product community. The PMO team can achieve much to dismantle it by empowering key figures in the project and product community and gaining leverage to future influence stubborn stakeholders.

6. Generate Short-Term Wins – short term wins also referred to as low hanging fruit, are important to accomplish. In most cases, change will take time and effort. Short-term wins encourage people to continue support the change initiative. Initial wins should be visible, explicit and closely linked to the change initiative. The PMO should identify areas that might generate quick wins, and move to capitalize on these opportunities. Significant areas of improvement that might yield quick wins may include:

1. A process to resolve critical resource over-allocation across a portfolio of projects;
2. Assisting in facilitation of cross-project conflict;

3. Composing a list of all the projects in the portfolio;

4. Facilitating strategic resource pool analysis and resource prioritization;

5. A rough order of magnitude analysis of the portfolio projects and their respective return on investment to enable project prioritization;

6. An issue management process that is both visible and comprehensive;

7. A useful status dashboard that can be used throughout the organization;

8. A WBS template general enough for most projects to use;

9. A common traceability matrix for scope management.

Note: PMOs should focus on balancing their efforts between creating short term wins and investing in long term objectives. Devoting too much effort for the short term wins might lead the PMO away from overall strategic realization. Some short term wins might actually become counter-productive from a strategic perspective.

7. Consolidate and Enable More Change – the previous step of plucking the low hanging fruits is vital in gaining further support for the next steps. Furthermore, it is necessary to aggregate the so far accomplished gains and arrange them in a cohesive value statement in order to build momentum and enable an environment for more and greater wins. This is not solely about positioning and marketing, rather it is a process of assessing the wins as part of the big picture. I have mentioned above that the PMO team should constantly ascertain that the short term wins are aligned with the vision and the value creation strategy. This step provides a useful context in which to validate the achievements indeed aligned.

8. Anchor New Approaches in Culture - leaders have to make the changes permanent by embedding them in the organizational culture, otherwise there is always the risk that changed behaviors, processes, tools etc will revert to the way they were. Long-lasting change becomes a part of the corporate culture through consistently and successfully changing behavior over sufficient period of time. One way to test if the change is successful is to ask users or stakeholders for the reason behind the execution of a certain (changed) activity. When the answer is: "that is the way we've always done that" then one can be sure that the change has been successful.

Beware: This is the third out of three neglected steps in PMO implementations.

Kotter does not claim that organizational change is simple to achieve; on the contrary he asserts that change is a complex process. He recognizes that many mistakes can be made along the way, actually even in successful change initiatives there are always surprises. Kotter's framework is a guideline, helping to avoid 'common mistakes' and to define the setting for successful implementation of the change.

PMO's staff and managers would benefit greatly from following Kotter's eight phases.

Summary table – Kotter 8 steps

Step	Action	New Behavior
1	Create a Sense Of Urgency	People start telling each other, "Let's go, we need to change things!"
2	Create a Coalition	A group powerful enough to guide a big change is formed and they start together well.
3	Create Vision and Strategy	The guiding team develops the right vision and strategy for the change effort.
4	Communicate the Change Vision	People begin to buy into the change, and this shows in their behavior.
5	Empower People	More people feel able to act, and do act, on the vision.
6	Generate Short-Term Wins	Momentum builds as people try to fulfill the vision, while fewer and fewer resist change.
7	Consolidate and Enable More Change	People make wave after wave of changes until the vision is fulfilled.
8	Anchor New Approaches in Culture	New and winning behavior continues despite the pull of tradition, turnover of change leaders etc.

Kotter's 8-Step Change Model for Successful Transformational Change

Source: Kotter and Cohen, The Heart of Change, p. 7.

According to Kotter and Cohen, successful change leaders find a problem or a solution to a problem and then show people using engaging and compelling situations to change behavior. They recommend a people-driven approach that helps people to see the reason for change. They argue that people change when they are shown the truth because this influences their feelings. That is, emotion is at the heart of change. We see, feel, change:

- See – Compelling and eye-catching situations are created to help show people what the problems are and how to resolve them;
- Feel – Visualizing ideas evokes a powerful emotional response that motivates people into action;
- Change – The new feelings change or reinforce behaviors that make people work harder to make a good vision reality. The change is more immediate but must be reinforced to keep up the momentum.

John Kotter is internationally known and widely regarded as the foremost expert on the topic of transformational leadership. He is the Konosuke Matsushita Professor of

Leadership, Emeritus at the Harvard Business School and a graduate of MIT and Harvard. John Kotter's international bestseller Leading Change—which outlines an actionable 8-step change model for implementing successful transformations—has become the bible for leaders around the world who want to achieve great results.

Chapter 8 – Reliably staying True to Value

A PMO that does not create value for the organization is a waste of money. However, how can value be defined for a PMO? The value of completing projects and delivering products is *implicitly* recognized. The PMO though does not execute projects and products. It is therefore vital to define what value is in relation to PMO activities. In order to do that we need to first better understand the value and benefits that projects contribute to the organization.

When searching for the definition of value in projects and products an interesting question arises. This question is one that some find hard to answer. The question is: What are projects good for?

Most answer: to implement the technology, to upgrade a product, to support the users, to put forth a reporting mechanism, and so on. These answers fall short of the big picture, for answering the question. In order to answer, one must acquire a broader view of the objectives of organizations. By and large, organizations are mostly in the business of making money. In this context, all projects are changes introduced to the organization to enable more creation of money. Without projects, organizations will continue doing more of the same and eventually will fade away. Therefore, projects and programs create value if in some way they contribute to the bottom line. That is not to say that a project to reduce pollution, or a project initiated to decrease poverty, or a project to support some educational objectives is not a value creator. However, as a rule, organizations deliver projects to enhance money making.

The PMO is creating value when it assists in completing more projects and products in a given time, thus making more money. In Truth, most PMOs achieve just the opposite – they interfere with value creation.

Beware: Let me repeat: the PMO is effective only when it helps the organization achieve more value adding projects at a given time. Intuitively this makes sense and as you're reading this statement you might be surprised at the considerable importance I'm assigning this very simple truth. However, organizations might understand this superficially and yet fail to grasp this genuinely. It is one thing to have it as part of the vision; it is another to assimilate **value added thinking** into everyday project and product management.

The reason behind is that organizations confuse between the means and the end. This is especially true for big organizations where project and product departments may be far away from the end customer. PMOs in these settings might mistake between creating value, and interfering with completing projects in a timely manner. In this respect a methodology in itself does not create value, a process does not create value, templates do not create value. Only completion of projects creates value. On top of that, the PMO is actually in a better position to assess value creation than the individual projects. The PMO, managing from the outside, is able to view an entire portfolio of projects and advise management which projects should be streamlined and which projects should be staggered, or terminated.

An effective PMO would not only ascertain that projects are completed according to plan, but also that the appropriate mix of projects is executed, and that the portfolio of projects is prioritized in a way which maximizes overall value.

Now that we have defiend what value is and how PMOs can create value, it is simple to assess activities performed by the PMO as promoting value creation or destroying value. In light of this, the single most important activity an effective PMO can perform is to create ubiquitous visibility of project and resource status, enabling prioritization and forward planning of resource allocation across a portfolio. There are several reasons for this:

1. The portfolio resource pool provides the leading constraint to overall value creation: as project completion in most scenarios is impacted by resource availability;
2. Resource is the money organization is paying to create the product; better resource allocation across a portfolio translates to more money;
3. Resource conflicts are the main hurdle in completing projects, most time-consuming conflicts between project managers amongst themselves and project managers and

resource managers are concerning resource allocation and prioritization;

4. In most organizations project managers do not have control over resources and cannot dictate resource allocation, even at times when they know that it is vital from a value perspective to have a specific resource allocated to their specific project;

5. Project managers have a partial view of the portfolio, are often biased in their decisions, and are limited to local rather than global optimized resource allocation;

6. Management lacks the bandwidth to understand resource interdependencies and when required to make a decision about resource allocation will most likely base its decision on ad hoc rules of thumb such as: who is the more senior project manager, which project manager yells louder, which project received the resources last time, which project is more important locally, which project does the VP of marketing need more, and other local semi optimization decisions which do not yield the best solution from a portfolio management perspective;

7. The project community, while immersed in the ad hoc and near future locally optimized resource allocations, is seldom concerned with the mid and long term resource availability across a portfolio and the opportunities for future value creation utilizing these resources.

The PMO would provide the highest value to the organization by managing resource allocation across a portfolio. The PMO would do that by continuously analyzing, prioritizing, and updating the resource pool and providing a global optimized view. All other PMO activities should be judged according to their contribution to management of the resource pool.

The project and product methodology in this perspective is a mutually accepted method to manage projects. A specific SDLC methodology for example enables the control of resource allocations across phases. This is not the only advantage of a software development lifecycle methodology. Other benefits of a SDLC as analyzed from the perspective of value creation and resource pool management may include:

1. Creation of a work breakdown structure template based on the SDLC which promotes unified resource estimating and budgeting;
2. Harmonization of project monitoring and controlling across the portfolio which enables an integrated reporting structure;
3. Comparison between projects in the portfolio as pertains to resource loading and future resource requirements, supporting prioritization of resources and projects;
4. Development of a historical database for estimating of efforts or of resource usage per work package or per project phase

assisting in current and future resource allocation across a portfolio.

In conclusion:

- Focusing on value is central to the implementation and management of a PMO.
- Value to the organization is created by completing projects and rolling out products.
- PMOs support value creation through decision-making from a portfolio management perspective.
- Projects that are beneficial to the portfolio and the organization are streamlined, while projects that are not beneficial to the portfolio and the organization are staggered or canceled.
- The portfolio resource pool provides the leading constraint to overall value creation, as project completion in most scenarios is impacted by resource availability.

Therefore, the greatest value a PMO can provide is the analysis, update and management of the resource pool. Other PMO activities should be judged according to the benefit they produce in accordance with the proper management of the resource pool.

Thinking Alert: I mention local and global optimization. In the context of project and products I imply the following. A certain business unit that is carrying out dozens of projects can prioritize them based on objective rules such as: prioritize and allocate constrained resource to the most profitable project in the portfolio. From the perspective of the department this will be the best solution for resource allocation. However since most organizations have cross functional dependencies, allocation of the resource to that specific project could yield less than optimal results from the companies perceptive. As we climb higher in the hierarchy, local decisions which seem perfectly justified, become questionable from the system perspective. Local optimization based on local rules, can and do, yield less than best results from a complete system viewpoint. The more global i.e. companywide approach to resource allocation across portfolios the better strategic results attained. Those of you who are reading this book and who operate PMOs within local departments and business units, don't fret, **even if you're contribution is local, it is still more effective and pertinent than having the project and resource managers decide on allocations based on arbitrary rules** (see the seven reason I have detailed above).

Chapter 9 – The Great and Simple Agile PMO – Delivering Value Easily

So far, this section has introduced two concepts:

1. PMO implementation is a change process and thus it is beneficial to use Kotter's framework for implementation of the change;

2. A PMO will prevail only if it is contributing value to the organization. Value in this context is the ability to make portfolio-based decisions regarding project prioritization and resource allocation.

The ninth chapter introduces the concept of the Agile PMO, which delivers only what is necessary at the appropriate time.

This chapter will revisit the case study and present the concept of the Agile PMO through a scenario. The scenario will include elements of chapter 7 and chapter 8.

Tom Jenkins, the newly appointed PMO manager convened his team. Xavier, Paula and Xing were eager to start work. Tom explained that the PMO rollout is a change process. He gave his team assignments around stakeholder analysis, mapping of communication requirements, and creation of the PMO newsletter. While the team was somewhat puzzled with these activities they moved to fulfill them nevertheless. Working with the stakeholders the team captured many complaints pertaining to the current way of work and gathered numerous requests for improvements. Eagerly awaiting their next meeting, which was held virtually by means of a videoconference, they prepared a list of proposed improvements. Xavier proposed to commence work on the work breakdown structure and the software development lifecycle. Paula suggested to update the risk register template and to implement a new tool for project scheduling. Xing reported that the stakeholders were keen on having a team collaboration tool and added that they are many resource conflicts which are not managed.

Tom listened carefully to his PMO team and empathized with their concerns. He then patiently detailed his vision of the PMO. While this was not the first time he discussed the vision, it was important that the team revisit the vision in light of their findings. He also instructed the team to communicate the vision continuously to the stakeholders during meetings. He further emphasized the importance of communicating through a newsletter to the global community. He moved to investigate with the team, which stakeholders were appearing to be powerful, interested and supportive to the cause of the PMO, and which were appearing to be opposing and would probably produce obstacles to the PMO implementation. He also offered his perspective concerning which activities might yield quick wins.

He then engaged the team in a discussion about value creation and how the PMO can provide value to the project and product community. He queried the team regarding the current status of the portfolio resource pool. It was evident from the team response that there was a resource pool in existence which was loosely managed, not centrally controlled, and not based on resource planned and actual efforts. Actually, in order to manage the resources on a global basis a new tool had to be implemented and more than 8000 resources had to be updated into the global tool. That was dire news indeed.

It seemed that in order to create value, the newly formed PMO had to immediately invest a huge sum in the procurement and implementation of a new software. Additionally, a new SDLC methodology had to be generated, updated processes had to be written and dozens of templates and work instructions developed.

This translated to a monumental undertaking and the team was at a loss regarding where to begin. They felt that it would be three years before they start producing value. One of them even suggested hiring a management consulting firm and recruiting five additional analysts to help with this huge undertaking. Once more Tom provided support to his team members, permitting them to air their concerns. Then he explained the concept of the Agile PMO.

He said that they did not have three years to create value; at most they had 100 days of grace before they were expected to produce some initial results. Xavier responded by offering to produce a new version of the risk register which may be not exactly what everyone needed but might make some stakeholders happy and buy the PMO some more precious time.

Tom gently rejected his offer, pointing out that a new risk register while useful, is not what an Agile PMO is about. The new risk register might add confusion and not support value creation and thus would be a waste of effort and time. This led to an extended period of silence and Tom suggested that the team would take a few days to think on how to proceed.

Three days later the team reconvened, Paula proposed an idea. She said that resource conflicts were abundant and that the most value added activity the PMO team could carry out, was to manage resources on a global scale. Tom commented that it was a good idea. Xing questioned the logic of this idea, saying that they are too many resources to manage. Xavier interjected and added that the tool which was in place was not able to support such a task. Paula said that they don't had to manage all resources, and maybe in an Agile PMO it was enough that they manage only what was needed to enable value creation. The other team members then listened attentively to her idea.

She explained that at this time they do not have a complete list of all projects executed globally and that should be their next task. Once they have such a list they would be able to assess project contribution from a portfolio perspective. Then they would be able to mediate between the different projects and assist management with making educated decisions pertaining to project prioritization based on the full list of projects in the global organization. Tom said that her idea was a good step in the right direction of being effective.

Eagerly, the team discussed how to carry out mapping of the projects. They defined a template to update the project list into and scheduled a meeting for the following week to review their results. Tom added that it is probably a good idea to present their findings in the newsletter and to continue stakeholders' assessments regarding support or opposition to the PMO activities.

During the team meeting the following week, it was evident that many pet projects existed, which were using resources without providing benefits to the portfolio. The team found that about 35% of projects which were redundant and probably unimportant to the portfolio of the company.

Tom said that this was a good example for an Agile PMO. Instead of discussing processes, tools and templates they were engaged in how to make the project and product community more effective. Xing then offered an idea; he said that he had noticed resource conflicts plaguing the projects in his region. He was convinced that these conflicts were occurring between important projects and it was very important to map all the resources allocated to these projects to resolve the conflicts. Resolving the conflicts would enable streamlining important projects, contributing to the portfolio. Xavier said that mapping and allocating all the resources in the region would be impossible as there are more than 800 resources in that specific region, and most of them do not report to timesheets on a regular basis. He added that in any case, the tool in place does not support these reporting requirements. Xing answered that he had given much thought and suggested that initially they map only the critical resources.

The team then deliberated what constitutes a critical resource. Tom offered his perspective and recommended they read an all-time bestseller on the subject of mapping of critical resources by the famous author and physicist Eli Goldratt: "Critical Chain Project Management". He said that true to the concept of the Agile PMO, they will identify critical resources. He estimated that only 3 to 5% of the total number of resources would prove to be critical. By following this line of reasoning, the team would quickly be able to allocate critical resources to prioritized projects enabling streamlining of the value creating projects from the portfolio perspective. Some quick and easy methods to identify critical resources in an organization can include:

1. Most often critical resources are self evident when examining the organization. By surveying the project community or polling for the purpose of identifying the critical resources, a

redundant short list consisting of the 2% to 4% of the total amount of resources is easily constructed. This short list is a useful starting point for the management of them. Based on it a pull mechanism to these critical resources can be defined;

2. Critical resources can also be identified by monitoring the projects in the organization and observing where queues are forming, where waiting times for projects are the longest, where most of the issues are emerging from, and so on. Usually these are the locations which involve critical resources;

3. It is also possible to consult the monitoring and controlling function (within the PMO for example) asking them where do they assist the most, which resources require the most rescheduling and which resources have a long buffer of work;

4. Other times, all that is necessary to identify critical resource is to join a few meetings and listen carefully to the names that keep popping up.

Clearly these are heuristic guidelines, rules of thumb to define critical resources; they are usually sufficient for identifying the critical resources. After identifying a short list, a pull mechanism for projects can be placed. Note that it is much better identifying a smaller list and increasing it if necessary than a long list that is most likely unmanageable.

One month later the PMO team was able to provide an almost complete list of projects in the global organization, along with the list of critical resources. These were the resources that impacted project completion. By closely managing loading of these resources, the PMO was able to provide and assist project managers and management with timely-based decisions concerning resource allocations. The PMO also suggested terminating **none=value=added projects** and transferring employees working on these projects to other projects which were creating value from the portfolio perspective. Three months after inception of the PMO, the impact of the PMO was already tangible:

1. More stakeholders were moving from neutral attitude to high support of the PMO activities;
2. The low hanging fruit of critical resource mapping provided quick wins which enabled more rigorous undertakings to complement the initial activities;
3. The newsletter was instrumental for conveying the message of value creation from the portfolio perspective.

With the support of Paula, Xavier and Xing, the vision set forth by Tom became a reality 20 months after PMO inception. Needless to say that within this time the PMO transformed into a strategic tool for portfolio decisions regarding future projects. The concept of the Agile PMO translated into a PULL mechanism of projects, whereby projects are selected based on resource pool status. This was opposed to the previous approach of a PUSH mechanism whereby all incoming projects were selected, which resulted in the clogging of the resource pool and thus hindering the streamlining effect and reducing the throughput of projects and the value achieved through project completion.

Naturally, with time a unified software development lifecycle was constructed along with relevant processes, templates, and then a new software tool for integrating information globally. The software tool was a natural evolution to the development effort of the PMO. The team understood that using a tool to create change is futile, and rather the tool should be implemented after a considerable amount of the change has been in place. The tool as such becomes a method to encapsulate the change into corporate culture.

In conclusion, the Agile PMO delivers what is needed at the time when it is required. The Agile PMO focuses on the most important value creating activities while keeping sight of the overall objective. This is in contrast to the development of all at once, which tends to be the initial expectation that is expressed by stakeholders. The PMO is not about tools, processes, or a methodology, rather it is about creating value.

Thinking Alert: Goldratt's critical chain project management is a great place to start when planning to roll out a value adding PMO. During workshops and seminars I notice that only few are familiar with the breakthrough ideas provided by Goldratt. Below are the key concepts from Goldratts book – Critical Chain Project Management.

Note that Goldratt rules enable a practical (not actual) global optimization of resource allocation, this has been the source for much debate in the Academic world since Multi Project Resource Constrained Scheduling is a NP (hard) problem and Goldratt's rule of thumb (heuristic) can't provide an optimal solution in certain situations. Having written that, I attest that for most reasonable scenarios, following Goldratt's ideas provides a beneficial context for PMOs to launch their value driven analysis and resource prioritization.

Critical Chain Project Management (CCPM) is a methodology for planning, executing and managing projects in single and multi-project environments. Critical Chain Project Management was developed by Dr Eli Goldratt and was first introduced to the market in his Theory of Constraints book "Critical Chain" in 1997. It was developed in response to many projects being dogged by poor performance manifested in longer than expected durations, frequently missed deadlines, increased costs in excess of budget, and substantially less deliverables than originally promised.

Problems with traditional project management

When planning for an upcoming project, estimates for task durations are required. In order for the plan to be treated as realistic, much time is spent ensuring estimates are accurate. Accurate estimates give us increased probability and high-confidence in the task completing on time. This allows additional safety time beyond the work content time required to be embedded within the task duration. The more safety in a task the more there is a tendency to behave in the following ways:

- Not starting the task until the last moment (Student Syndrome)
- Delaying (or pacing) completion of the task (Parkinson's Law)
- Cherry picking tasks

As a result, the safety which was included at the planning stage is wasted and, if "Murphy" strikes and problems do occur, tasks over-run.

In addition Management forces (for intuitive but invalid reasons) people to work on more than one task at once – creating multitasking. This drives people to switch between tasks leading them to elongate time estimates in planning and further waste the embedded task safety in execution.

Resources working on tasks also naturally resist reporting any early finishes. If an early finish is reported, the estimate for the task is recognized as too long. When a similar task on a different project is estimated, the initial response will be to again use a worst case duration. This will inevitably be challenged as the similar task was finished early last time. Increased pressure will be placed on the resource to accept a shorter estimate this time. The risk is that this, shorter estimate will not offer sufficient safety to the project should a problem occur. Hence resources ensure that sufficient safety is always embedded in each task estimate and the entire safety is used in execution of the task. This game is played by management and resources!

In summary, delays to tasks are passed on to the entire project however; benefits from tasks finishing early are rarely passed on to the same project.

The traditional tools used to manage projects; Critical Path Method (CPM), Program Evaluation and Review Technique (PERT), Gantt, Prince Etc. do not address the misuse of embedded safety and consequently the behaviors they drive.

Critical Chain Project Management

Critical Chain Project Management addresses these issues in the following ways.

Planning

Critical Chain - the Critical Chain is defined as the longest chain [not path] of dependent tasks. In this case, 'dependent' refers to resources and resource contention across tasks/projects as well as the sequence and logical dependencies of the tasks themselves. This differs from the Critical Path Method.

Estimations – To reduce the behaviors and time wasting associated with having too much embedded safety, Critical Chain Project Management recommends that task estimates are cut to half the length of a "normal" duration.

Safety – Critical Chain Project Management uses safety **'Buffers' to manage the impact of variation and uncertainty around projects**. The safety at a task level is aggregated and moved to strategic points in the project flow. There are three types of buffer/strategic points necessary to ensure the project has sufficient safety:

Project Buffer – A project buffer is inserted at the end of the project network between the last task and the completion date. Any delays on the longest chain of dependant tasks will consume some of the buffer but will leave the completion date unchanged and so protect the project. The project buffer is typically recommended to be half the size of the safety time taken out, resulting in a project that is planned to be 75% of a "traditional" project network.

Feeding Buffers – suggested PMO role – delays on paths of tasks feeding into the longest chain can impact the project by delaying a subsequent task on the Critical Chain. To protect against this, feeding buffers are inserted between the last task on a feeding path and the Critical Chain. The feeding buffer is typically recommended to be half the size of the safety time taken out of the feeding path.

Resource Buffers – suggested PMO role – Resource buffers can be set alongside of the Critical Chain to ensure that the appropriate people and skills are available to work on the Critical Chain tasks as soon as needed.

Execution – suggested PMO role

Priorities - All resources on a project are given clear and aligned priorities relating to the 'health' of the Critical Chain relative to its associated buffer and hence the project as a whole. A resource with more than one task open should normally be assigned to complete any task jeopardizing any projects Critical Chain before completing any feeding path task.

Completion – resources on a task are encouraged to follow the 'roadrunner' approach. When there is work available it should be progressed at the fastest possible speed (without compromising quality) until completed. Tasks are not left partially complete to remove the temptation to multitask. As task duration estimates have reduced safety they drive resources to meet the more "aggressive" durations and limit the behaviors of Student Syndrome and Parkinson's Law.

Review – suggested PMO role

Buffer Management – the amount each buffer is consumed relative to project progress tells us how badly the delays are effecting our committed delivery date. If the variation throughout the project is uniform then the project should consume its project buffer at the same rate tasks are completed. The result is a project completed with the buffer fully consumed on the day it was estimated and committed. Project Managers determine the corrective actions necessary to 'recover' buffer time at points in the project where the buffer consumption is occurring faster than the project is progressing.

Remaining duration – tasks are monitored on their remaining duration, not their percentage complete. Resources report upon tasks in progress based on the number of days they estimate until the task will be complete. If the remaining duration stays static or increases, then Project Managers and Resource Managers "watching the buffers" know exactly where a blockage or potential delay is occurring and can take decisive action quickly to recover.

In the next chapter, which has been added to this book later, we review the concepts of integrating the Agile PMO with Agile/Scrum approach/methods. It is worthwhile to differentiate between Goldratt's approach which aims at global optimization, and Agile which is a set of approaches that focus on local optimization. Actually it makes absolute sense from a system perspective to follow the suggestions described in the next chapter for the Agile PMO fulfilling an integrative role – connecting top down global methods such as critical chain with local Agile optimizations.

Chapter 10 – Interfacing between Linear Waterfall and Agile Approaches

As mentioned in the preface to the second edition, this chapter depicts the best practice approach for integrating Agile approaches and specifically Scrum development, with traditional overarching linear approaches, specifically waterfall methodology. The agile PMO, properly defined, can be positioned to secure Agile-Scrum benefits while maintaining the necessary overarching control.

The challenge

Over the last two decades, various Agile approaches have been introduced and practiced. Of these, in last 5 to 7 years, Scrum has gained the most popularity resulting from a combination of simplicity, ease of use, and effective public relations. Scrum success in software development organizations has been a powerful driver for roll outs across products, industries and businesses. As described, this was exacerbated by a focused marketing effort from Scrum evangelists. Unfortunately, most of these organizations were not structured in a way that supports the Agile-Scrum approach and methods. Even more so, scrum in its raw and pure form is not suitable for the majority of organizations.

The first wave of failed Agile-Scrum implementations brought about an even stricter admonition, based on an unwavering belief from Scrum zealots. The main assertion has been that failed implementations are a result of partial embracing of the true scrum spirit and the full benefits of the approach can only be attained if the entire organization is reengineered. This fanatical attitude left many project teams across organizations big and small, struggling with their already idealistic implementations. Some have been figuring out on their own, how to combine the contemporary and traditional worlds. Other teams have completely abandoned the Agile-Scrum concepts reverting back to the traditional linear waterfall approach and method. Yet other teams, ridden with guilt, manage Scrum by name only, and hiss vehemently at any project management proponent who is unfortunate enough to advise on re-embracing Agile in a more cognizant approach.

The concepts which are presented and embodied in Agile-Scrum are too good to be ignored; however implementing it outside pure software development requires adaptation.

Complex scenarios for Agile

The main hurdle in achieving the benefits of Agile- Scrum outside software development is integrating it with existing control mechanisms. These control mechanisms are stipulated due to various organizational prerequisites and are normally actualized by using the Linear Waterfall approach and methodology. Four of these typical organizational prerequisites are depicted below:

- Big global corporates – in these hierarchical matrix organizations, top down portfolio control is the rule of the day. The free spirited agile approach has a tough time adjusting to the rigorous controls. Specifically the inherent Agile plan-free concepts, make Agile-Scrum difficult for the organization to swallow.
- Highly regulated industries – some industries are required by compliance and governance bodies to have a strict binding control mechanism. These can be for example medical equipment, aircraft, and pharmaceuticals research and product development business units. While individual teams might operate Agile-Scrum, the development process must follow a rigid Linear Waterfall approach method for traceability and governance.
- Complex predefined products – some integrated products which include both hardware, software, imbedded and more are developed as a contract with an end customer under a predefined set of requirements. In these cases the degree of requirement flexibility is small, though larger than what is anticipated initially. The concept of a fully flexible backlog of Agile-Scrum suffers considerably in these cases.
- Generic IT departments – much of the daily and weekly activities in maintenance driven IT departments is ad hoc. Changes to the daily schedules are numerous and immediate. Constant interferences in the teams work are the norm. The

concept of time boxing and no interference is difficult to maintain in these situations.

Naturally – many times the four discrete categories detailed above, actually mix; so it is common to find a complex product in a global big corporate which is required to comply with firm regulation.

Based on practical experience, the recommended method to tackle these scenarios and others is by empowering the Agile PMO to act as an enabler, driver and translator between the emerging Agile-Scrum teams and the Linear Waterfall elements.

Refer to the table below for specific guidelines

The Agile PMO – leading the hybrid organization - guidelines

Scenario	Challenge	Possible solution	Comments	Insights
Big global corporates	Strict controls manifested in Linear Waterfall	The Agile PMO is the buffer between Agile-Scrum teams and the Linear control	Burn down charts are translated to phases for control; Requirement traceability done by PMO architect; Agile PMO maintains the	Product owners can be part of the Agile PMO; Project initiating and closing managed by the PMO

Scenario	Challenge	Possible solution	Comments	Insights
			dictionary between sprint planning, execution and the phase gating mechanism	
Highly regulated industries	Strict compliance and paper trail requirement, including product risk analysis	The Agile PMO is also resourced by administrative staff to ensure compliance with regulations	Product risk is managed on a lifecycle view with members of the Scrum-Agile team; Backlog populated by Non-functional yet critical requirements and owned by the Agile PMO; Agile PMO staff maintains traceability of these requirements; Necessary documentation is part of the backlog	The added administrative effort handled by the PMO is compensated by the increased velocity of the Agile teams. Administrative PMO staff can also be non-functional product owners to ensure compliance aspects

Scenario	Challenge	Possible solution	Comments	Insights
Complex predefined products	Limited flexibility in product scope tends to deteriorate Agile implementations to Agile by name only; Also, hardware elements of product can't be performed in an Agile approach	The Agile PMO owns the backlog interfacing with the various components of product development – managing a hybrid Agile-Linear project	This is probably the most difficult and tricky scenario to tackle; It requires technical as well as leadership propensity and know-how; Experience shows that by investigating creatively – Agile concepts can be implemented in rigid hardware development environments Also – rigid product requirements still allow usually 20% flexibility	the most value added can be reaped in this scenario by developing a customized mixed approach; Agile stage deliveries can be used to increase flexibility; Concepts of incremental deliveries may sometimes not be achievable in all product aspects
Scenario	Challenge	Possible solution	Comments	Insights
Generic IT departments	Constant changes to	The Agile PMO substitutes the	Many disheartened IT	Noticeably, Kanban works

	team's work, inability to see the big picture due to ad-hoc work interfering; missing a true product owner	product owner role in acting as a buffer to oncoming requests also protecting effort to reasonable levels	departments have become bitter when trying to use Agile to their development and ongoing work; the result has been fatigue laden team, viewing Agile as a vicious manipulation to increase output without genuine management support; more than a single project management approach can be practiced	better for these environments; Time boxing still makes sense, however a certain predefined buffer for ad-hoc work should be built into each sprint; Sprint durations should be flexible

Important best practices to remember that go hand in hand with the Agile PMO:

- Implementing Agile-Scrum as a restricting admonition is exploiting the adaptive nature of Agile;
- There is no one right way – no one size fits them all;
- There is no silver bullet – you can create what works for you;
- Being agile and adaptive also allows being flexible with how one uses the methods, process and Methodology;
- Time boxing is great as long as you are flexible to change the durations of the time box if necessary;
- Sometimes the client isn't directly available, in these cases marketing and product management are a proper alternate;

Arbitrary rules don't complete projects, people do! Empower your team and yourself to choose the appropriate mix of approaches that enable product delivery.

Summarizing - with the emerging of Agile approaches and specifically Scrum methods new opportunities have become apparent. Integrating them into an existing control structure – typically presented by a waterfall lifecycle – can be frustrating. We have defined a new key player – the Agile PMO which can be positioned to create a transformation / translation layer between the approached and methods, contributing to higher success levels of these integrations.

Thank you for your time, I hope you found this guide useful.

I have read many books about PMOs and have seen many implementations, most of them failed. I offered my perspective on how to create a long-lasting value driven PMO. We have covered the prime approach for creating and leading a value driven PMO. Organizations which follow these guidelines benefit from extraordinary results in project completion, in benefits received, customer satisfaction, and in low employee attrition. Following these guidelines will enable you to lead your PMO to success.

I wish you best of luck in your PMO implementation efforts.

Thinking alert: Remember where we started? Most PMOs fail because they aren't focusing correctly. They might be doing the following:

1. Discussing tools before process
2. Selecting a process before methodology
3. Investing time in a methodology before leading the stakeholders and creating a strong support group for the PMO

Instead they must remember that the goal of each and every PMO is one: to create value. A PMO creates value when and only when it enables educated fact-based decisions regarding resource allocation across projects, programs and portfolios. If subsequent to one year of inception, the PMO cannot provide an up-to-date accurate view of resource allocation then it has failed in the single most important role that a PMO has in the organization.

In order to do that the PMO should follow the three concepts presented in this book:

- Implement the PMO as a change initiative following Kotter's 8 steps
- Focus on value creation from a portfolio and organization perspective
- Deliver value inclemently and adaptively facilitating constant alignment with the vision and the strategic objectives
- Integrate approaches and methods and in doing so assume the role of a mediator, translator, and aggregator

I'll be happy to answer your questions. Feel free to contact me @ sapir@sapir-cs.com

You'll find more about Agile and the product owner in Agile Product Owner Secrets Valuable Proven Results for Agile Management Revealed - a free chapter is offered just here:

Free Glimpse: Breakthrough! Being Agile – The Product Owner as a Change Agent

The product owner acts as a catalyst of change in the organization – enabling value creation through projects and products. He creates the required link between how the business would look like in the future and the current state. The product owner is a key facilitator within the organization in bridging the client and the business community with the Agile development team. Most of what a product owner performs can be defined in the broader sense as:

1. Creating and increasing value for the business
2. Eliminating and reducing costs for the business

The product owner is required to identify business needs and determine solutions to business challenges. We can characterize the role description of the product owner as related to the above tasks into several key responsibilities. The product owner needs to:

1. Mine for and create epics that guide the business towards value creation and cost savings;
2. Plan and maintain epics, themes and user stories;
3. Elicit epics, themes and user stories;
4. reach consensus and understanding of epics themes and user stories between the business and the Agile development team;

5. Focus on user stories according to specific guidelines such as INVEST (This is an acronym regarding the development of user stories they should be: Independent, Negotiable, Valuable, Estimable, Small, Testable);

6. Communicate and collaborate continuously.

As the product owner is the focal point for strategic and tactical product management he collaborates with many stakeholders and must communicate with all of them. Specifically the product owner interacts with the business community and the Agile development teams on a regular basis. He should also communicate with management in making sure that business objectives are indeed captured in themes and epics.

On any single Agile development effort the product owner:

1. Elicits user stories, making them INVESTabile;

2. Analyzes them with the team;

3. Provides feedback to the business community;

4. Communicates continuously while prioritizing user stories;

5. Monitors user stories to their respective epics and themes;

6. Supports the Agile development teams throughout the Sprint – providing clarifications where needed;

7. Approves and accepts the developed features at the end of the Sprint;

8. Maintains a rudimentary or full-fledged traceability of user stories to business, to epics and themes, and to any other relevant criteria that he has defined.

This guide emphasizes the product owner's activities, specifically the communication aspect of his role. Communication is a key differentiator in the product owner's effectiveness and most often an aspect in which product owners are lacking the necessary know how. This in turn impacts negatively the product owner's performance. Emphasis is given to the elicitation of user stories; since product owners are usually gathering the stories instead of eliciting them.

The main difference between gathering and eliciting is: *Elicitation* is an analytical, free flowing communication and collaboration effort which fits well with Agile development as described in the Agile manifesto. *Gathering* is a passive activity with little invested analysis. When a product owner is a gatherer he is actually no more than an administrator...

To summarize the points above: it is vital that the product owner understands the context in which he is working, the tools that he can use while performing the work, and the essence of what it means to be a product owner in an effective Agile product development environment.

Improved insight - Customer Needs – The Point for Effective Communication

The product owner constantly communicates and collaborates both with the business community and with Agile development teams. Communicating is the basis for collaborating , without being able to communicate effectively, collaboration cannot exist.

Communicating has several goals:

1. Letting others know of something;
2. Asking for feedback from others;
3. Convincing others;
4. Proactively building relationships.

In the above process of communication; personal, cultural, intercultural, and language barriers exist. The product owner should be cognizant of these barriers and understand that the same message can be perceived differently than anticipated as well as differently by various groups and teams of stakeholders.

An effective product owner understands that messages are received, deciphered and perceived differently by others since they have individual and distinct perception filters. Examples of filter categories can be:

1. Values-personal – values impact the way a message is perceived;

2. Interests – a specific team member interest in a certain user story can impact the way he estimates that story;

3. Expectations – different expectations result in different levels of collaboration;

4. Past experience – past experience can alter how people accept a certain message and respond to it. This for example can result in different understanding of the same user story to be developed.

When communicating we are subjective, we move away from messages that conflict with our ideas and beliefs. We tend to hear just what we want to hear, we usually pay more attention to things that interest us. Our past experience impact and biases us, emotions and psychological states impact how we perceive a message and how we communicate. Taking into account these obstacles to mutually effective communication, it is vital that the product owner spend time both when eliciting the user stories and also in conveying them to the team. During the Sprint planning meeting or for that matter any other Agile process which includes detailing the user stories to the development team, care should be given to feedback loops and the clear understanding of what is required to be developed.

When discussing the user story with the Agile development team for example, it is not sufficient to read out loud the user story cards, the product owner should actively ask for feedback to assure understanding concerning the specific story. It is useful to add graphics, diagrams, illustrations, and mind maps to emphasize the understanding.

Key message:

I probably cannot emphasize enough how important this is in an Agile environments. Since Agile is scarce in formal documentation the clear and concise understanding of what is required to be developed during the collaborative process between product owner and the Agile development team, is key to the Agile development process. Without the clear understanding of what needs to be developed the team might be investing efforts in the wrong direction. Thus, it can be a very *efficient* Sprint i.e. speedy and producing the stated results; however it will also be an *ineffective* Sprint meaning that the results received are not the ones which were required.

This constant feedback and communication loop between the product owner and the business community, and between the product owner and the development team is key to successful product development in Agile environment. It is also a key element in any product development environment; however as mentioned before – the typical lack of formal documents in Agile necessitates the constant communication and collaboration, clarifying expectations and interests during Agile development.

I suggest that all product owners participate in communication skills training, learn strategies in developing their skills, and enhance their facilitation techniques, which is on top of reading this useful book.

A practical approach to handle the communication barriers is to make sure that:

1. One knows the communication objective ahead of time;
2. Remains cognizant during a communication interaction and analyze the specific situation from both the communicator and the receiver perspectives.
3. Remains aware of the restrictions imposed by the environment.
4. Establishes and promotes a multi-way feedback loop;
5. Is able to communicate in more than one method: i.e. pictures, drawing, diagrams and prototypes. These are great tools to enhance communication.

The product owner's core competencies are facilitation, communication and leadership skills. Effective product owners are able to:

1. Listen;
2. Emphasize;
3. Facilitate meetings;
4. Handle tough communication and conflict management situations;

5. Be effective presenters;

6. Lead product related business decisions and openly discuss them with the Agile development team;

Negotiate, mediate and influence between the Agile development teams and the business community.

Want to learn more about key concepts of the product owner? **Agile Product Owner Secrets Valuable Proven Results for Agile Management Revealed,** available on Amazon.com, and in all other Amazon stores close to you.

Before you go

Did you enjoy this book? You might find **these great titles** of interest:

Satisfaction Guaranteed!

Absolutely unique guides on Team leadership – we have the following amazing practical guides to help you out:

Six Secrets of powerful teams Guaranteed to make a remarkable impact

Bestseller!

With this book you will achieve remarkable results:
** Your team will perform better
** You will effectively motivate your team better
** You will understand how to influence the team members to make them work well
It doesn't stop here – this book is relevant to ANY team – families, friends and any interaction that is more than just YOU!

Influence without authority? Wait no longer!

I know, you are searching for the ultimate method to build rapport with your stakeholders and emerge as a great influencer, aren't you? Once you finish

Business & Project Teams Management Winning influence without authority

You will secure personalized practical advice relevant to YOU; why not sample a look-inside NOW.

Bestseller!

Simple - 3 Proven Fundamentals - Unlocking the Secrets of Leadership and Influence!

* Imagine that you master the magic of influence and get people to do what you want?
* Imagine that you have a clear path of how to accomplish it.
* We have some good news and some bad news: The good news is that with the revealed secrets in this practical book you can quickly learn how to influence and lead.
* These are proven methods that have been tested by the author in his global professional experience.
* The bad news is that you have missed many opportunities by not reading this book so far.
* After you read this book you will not understand how you ever lived without the amazing knowledge within.

Free Glimpse: Secrets of powerful teams - Revealing ideas of NLP and the use of words

You'll find more about teams and team leading in: **The six secrets of powerful teams** a free chapter is offered just here:

The ongoing challenges of creating the magical bond between team members in small and big endeavors can be elusive. What more, in the last few decades it has become increasingly challenging, since we have been moving from emphasis on social skills and communities to technical and managerial skills, as a result the lore concerning the magic of teams has been lost.

When I'm facilitating workshops for business professionals, project managers in software development, seminars for finance and IT professionals, consulting with marketing and supply chain experts, I am surprised to witness their low propensity for soft skills literacy. They know the hard aspects of what needs to be done, however they remain clueless when required to lead the teams that help them accomplish the required objectives.

As most of these teams are cross functional in a matrix organization, it is likely that the leaders and managers of these teams do not necessarily have direct hierarchical control over the team members. Requesting deliverables from the team members becomes challenging. Even when the managers do have hierarchical power, the contemporary concepts of empowerment and motivation prevail, making direct commands unpopular to say the least. Yet again requesting fulfillment of the objectives and deliverables becomes tricky. It is quite remarkable that simple concepts for creating positive interactions outside the business world are hardly ever used within business and project teams.

In order to lead through the challenges of both collocated and virtual teams we can use concepts from Neurolinguistic programming (NLP). It is a powerful technique with proven results.

We will explore only a fraction of what NLP is about, specifically several words that are used redundantly in almost each and every team interaction. These words are mostly negative, yet common in team interactions, create noise in the communication, confuse the message, and carry a baggage of ill-considered meanings.

The first word we will examine is - Try

The first word that is used quite often without understanding the implication is: **Try**.

For example: 'we will try running this test next week' or 'please try to have the results by Wednesday' or even 'I tried really hard'.

Try - masks the intent and carries an element of implicit failure within the message. As Yoda said, you either do it or you don't there is no try. Either you're going to run the tests next week or you're not going to run them next week. When you're saying that: you are going to try to run them next week, most like you're not going to do it. When I'm telling you: please try to have the results by Wednesday, I'm actually saying that it is fine that they'll come in by Thursday or Friday or even next month.

Let us look at an email example written by Mark, a team leader:

> We have indeed defined a way of work, but we also defined a process for completion of tasks, that we should **try** to stick to.

What is Mark saying? Did we define a process just so we should try to stick to it? Or did we define a process that we must stick to? By using try, Mark undermines his authority as a team leader; he defined a process so that the team members will follow it.

The abundant use of the word try in many teams, both co-located and virtual, is a sign of fear that both leaders and team members have of stepping up and asking for commitment and responsibility.

Bottom line - drop the TRY it does not add anything to the communication!

The second word we will examine is - Should

The second word that is used quite often without understanding the implication is: **Should**.

'Should' has a flavor of admonition, guilt, and manipulation, especially when other people are using it; by blurting out-loud a general statement with the word 'should'.

For example: "you should always finish what you're eating and never leave anything on the plate". Also: "this should have been completed by now". And yet another: "you should not get up before the manager has left".

Let us look at a meeting, where Tina – a production lead, is saying:

> Tina answers: "we **should** focus on production levels as this is what is driving the transfer to production, trust me I've been here and have seen these projects many times

In this case Tina is using 'should' to reprimand the team and also to have it her way by defining an imaginary rule and enforcing it upon the team. Actually what Tina is saying: "I want to focus on production levels". Many times people use should instead of 'I want', this is the case with parents and children. The admonition of: "you should be nice" is actually saying: "I want you to be nice".

Observe the power and direct impact of the second sentence as opposed to using 'should'. People use the word should to mask their wish or need. Instead of directly stating what they want, they construct a stipulation without naming a person responsible for carrying it out.

In families we often hear such a 'should' sentence: "the lawn should be cut". This is indirect communication that with time can create resentment. Actually the person would be better off asking directly what he wants to happen: "please can you cut the lawn now", is a much better question. Notice that this question can lead into conflict as the other person might rebel and disagree. By using 'should' we are avoiding the conflict between our wishes and the other person's wishes. The truth is that the conflict **is not avoided**; rather as the communication is not direct it is unclear what the person wants the other person to perform. **The conflict thus is exacerbated and not mitigated**. The extensive use of 'should' stipulations occurs in families, in couples, and naturally also in teams.

Monitor the 'shoulds' in your teams, they are barriers to effective communication and reduce the potential power of the team.

The third word we will examine is - Why

The third word that is used quite often without understanding the implication is: **Why**.

Why carries a sense of blame to it. for example: "why did you break the glass?" One can see that the usage of 'why' here is not about receiving an answer but more about rebuking for the actual breaking of the glass, since there is not a good answer for this question. A wisecrack answer might be: "because I like to see you get mad..."

actually, it is just the right answer for a question with the word 'why' and often an answer we receive from teenagers for 'WHY' questions.

For example, at the same meeting, Ashley the project manager is answering:

> Ashley tries to gain control back and asks Tina: "**why** do you think this is now relevant for our meeting? Let's try to get back on our planned agenda!"

In this case Ashley is blaming Tina by asking her the question. Ashley would have been better off saying: "Tina, I would like to revert to our defined agenda, I think these are relevant issues for another meeting".

The word 'why' carries guilt and finger-pointing into our team communications. It is better that we leave it out of our messages as it doesn't have any positive impact on what we are saying. Rather it is clearer to state what we want to achieve or alternatively ask information gathering questions using the word 'how'.

For example Ashley might ask: "Tina, can you please explain how these figures impact the transfer to operations?"

Notice that while 'why' structures a closed ended question, 'how' questions are open-ended and investigate as to the process that led to a certain consequence.

The 'whys' don't contribute to clear communication instead they add guilt and finger-pointing, drop them!

Maybe you are looking for Breakthrough and Daring personal Growth – this guide works like Magic:

Silent Influencing - Employing Powerful Techniques for Influence and Leadership

Bestseller!

Are you tired of not getting your message across? Of not being heard? Of having your boss always ignoring you and your spouse not caring what you think?

Silent influencing is THE guide for you. It will enable you to change how you interact with others, how to influence them and how to lead to results. With Silent Influencing you will succeed.

It includes world proven techniques and an easy to implement approach; Silent Influencing has in ONE DAY REACHED AMAZON AMONG 200 ALL TIME BESTSELLER KINDLE FREE LIST.

More interested in High-Tech project and portfolios? We have a unique guide – the most value for money – Agile book there is. It is a real Bonanza

Agile Product Owner Secrets- Valuable Proven Results for Agile Management Revealed

Proven and Tested Advice for the Agile and SCRUM Product Owner

* Pioneering! The author is absolutely forth coming, saying in a clear voice what everyone is avoiding! The agile scrum king is Naked! with remarkable clarity the shortcoming of agile and scrum in the Big boys - corporate business are displayed.
* You know it is the truth? don't you? You have witnessed it yourself in your company! *I will reliably guide you on what others don't tell you, the business analyst come product owner - making the product owner a powerful tool from a strategic perspective!*
* Maybe you are afraid to take the first step? Aren't you? You have

heard others experiences with Agile and are unsure...let me introduce you to how it works easily and quickly.

* Astonishing! I know what you are thinking - how is this never told before? Like you I was also dazzled by the powerful assertions however I quickly realized from practical and focused engagements that it just doesn't work in the pure way - in real life there has to be adjustments!

* The Powerful Product Owner is for *any project and product practitioner and team wishing to make use of emerging Agile High Tech concepts with Reliable waterfall tested concepts for Survival in the business*

***

Made in the USA
San Bernardino, CA
13 November 2013